ALTERNATOR BOOKS™

NATIVE HUNTING AND FISHING

Practicing Traditions and Defending Treaty Rights

KATRINA M. PHILLIPS

Lerner Publications ◆ Minneapolis

For Leo and Max

Content consultant: Jill Doerfler

Lerner Publications Company
An imprint of Lerner Publishing Group, Inc.
241 First Avenue North
Minneapolis, MN 55401 USA

For reading levels and more information, look up this title at www.lernerbooks.com.

Main body text set in Aptifer Sans LT Pro Medium.
Typeface provided by Linotype AG.

Designer: Athena Currier

Map illustration on page 14 by Laura K. Westlund.

Library of Congress Cataloging-in-Publication Data

Names: Phillips, Katrina M., author.
Title: Native hunting and fishing : practicing traditions and defending treaty rights / Katrina M. Phillips.
Description: Minneapolis : Lerner Publications, [2025] | Series: Native rights (Alternator Books) | Includes bibliographical references and index. | Audience: Ages 8–12 | Audience: Grades 4–6 | Summary: "Many Native American nations rely on their hunting and fishing rights. But the United States government has not always upheld these rights. Readers discover how Native nations are defending their rights"— Provided by publisher.
Identifiers: LCCN 2024014976 (print) | LCCN 2024014977 (ebook) | ISBN 9798765646908 (library binding) | ISBN 9798765661697 (paperback) | ISBN 9798765656679 (epub)
Subjects: LCSH: Indians of North America—Social life and customs—Juvenile literature. | Indians of North America—Hunting—Law and legislation—United States—Juvenile literature. | Indians of North America—Fishing—Law and legislation—United States—Juvenile literature. | Indians of North America—Legal status, laws, etc.—Juvenile literature.
Classification: LCC E98.S7 P45 2025 (print) | LCC E98.S7 (ebook) | DDC 342.7308/72—dc23/eng/20240605

LC record available at https://lccn.loc.gov/2024014976
LC ebook record available at https://lccn.loc.gov/2024014977

Manufactured in the United States of America
1-1010985-53131-7/30/2024

TABLE OF CONTENTS

INTRODUCTION
FIGHTING FOR OUR RIGHTS

In the nineteenth century, the United States government forced many Native nations to give up their lands. The government promised to protect Native nations in exchange for these lands. The US government also promised that Native peoples would still have the right to hunt and fish on these lands. But between the 1950s and the 1970s, the US took away the rights of more than one hundred Native nations across the US. This policy is known as termination and was an effort to force assimilation on Native peoples.

One of the affected nations was the Confederated Tribes of Siletz Indians. Termination tried to strip Native peoples of their cultures. It would also strip Native nations of their rights as sovereign nations. But Native peoples such as the Siletz stood up for themselves, their nations, and their rights, including their rights to hunt and fish.

Siletz chair Delores Pigsley works to protect traditional hunting and fishing rights in 2011.

The Confederated Tribes of Siletz Indians were restored as a nation in 1977. But there was a catch. The US government would only restore the Siletz as a nation if they gave up their rights to hunt and fish. The Siletz did not feel as if they had a choice. So they agreed to give up their traditional rights.

But the Siletz pressed for a return of their rights. They took their case to Congress. In 2023 the US House of Representatives passed a bill supporting the traditional hunting and fishing rights of the Confederated Tribes of Siletz Indians.

CHAPTER 1
The Land Provides

Historically, Native peoples provided for themselves by hunting, fishing, and gathering. Peoples who lived near oceans often built canoes that could handle the deep ocean waters. They caught animals such as whales and larger fish. Others fished in rivers and lakes. Some gathered shellfish such as mussels and oysters along the shore.

Native Food Sources

Native peoples from nations in the Great Plains hunted for animals such as deer and bison. Bison were essential to life on

Citizens of the Makah Tribe set out on a whale hunt in 1998.

the plains. Native peoples ate bison meat. They made clothing and tipi covers from the bison hides. Other Native peoples hunted smaller game such as rabbits, turkeys, and quail.

Native nations also grew crops such as corn, squash, and beans. The Ojibwe and other nations around the Great Lakes harvested manoomin. *Manoomin* means "the food that grows on water." It is known as wild rice in English. Native peoples relied on the animals and the land to provide everything they needed to live. In return, they expressed their thanks and did not take more than they needed.

A citizen of Ohkay Owingeh uses a hunting bow in 2023.

Bison and Beavers

People from Europe started coming to what is now North America in the seventeenth century. They didn't have the same respect for the land and animals. Traders, explorers, and settlers saw the land and the animals as resources that could be exploited. They killed so many beavers in the fur trade era that beavers almost went extinct.

REFLECT

Native peoples often only hunted and fished enough to provide for their communities. How was this different from how settlers often hunted and fished?

White settlers stand with a pile of bison skulls in 1892.

In the nineteenth century, the US government paid hunters to kill as many bison as they could. Because of this, bison herds almost became extinct. As settlers pushed farther and farther west, they made changes to the land and used many resources. Native peoples had a more difficult time getting what they needed to survive.

CHAPTER 2
The Treaty Era

As settlers moved west, they wanted lands for farming. The US pressured Native nations to sign treaties. These documents forced Native nations to cede most of their lands to the US government. Native nations kept access to the ceded lands for hunting, fishing, and gathering. The US government often promised to provide food, supplies, health care, education, and money to Native nations in exchange. But the government often didn't keep these promises. Native peoples were forced to live on smaller and smaller portions of land called reservations.

Treaty Rights

Native nations across the US stood up for their rights. They wanted to exercise the hunting and fishing rights protected by treaties. In 1837 Wisconsin territorial governor Henry Dodge wanted Ojibwe people to sign away their rights to millions of acres of land. More than one thousand Ojibwe

An 1868 treaty between the Nez Perce Tribe and the US government

Chief Eshkibagikoonzhe is known for his powerful speeches.

people traveled to Fort Snelling. It was a military post in what is now the state of Minnesota.

At the treaty negotiations, Ojibwe leaders told Dodge that they wanted to protect their rights to hunt, fish, and gather on these lands. Chief Eshkibagikoonzhe, also called Flat Mouth, told Dodge that Ojibwe people could not live without access to those lands and waters. The US agreed that the Ojibwe would keep their rights to hunt, fish, and gather on lands they ceded to the US. So Ojibwe leaders signed. They also agreed to treaties in 1842 and 1854 that protected their hunting and fishing rights.

OJIBWE LAND CEDED IN TREATIES BY YEAR

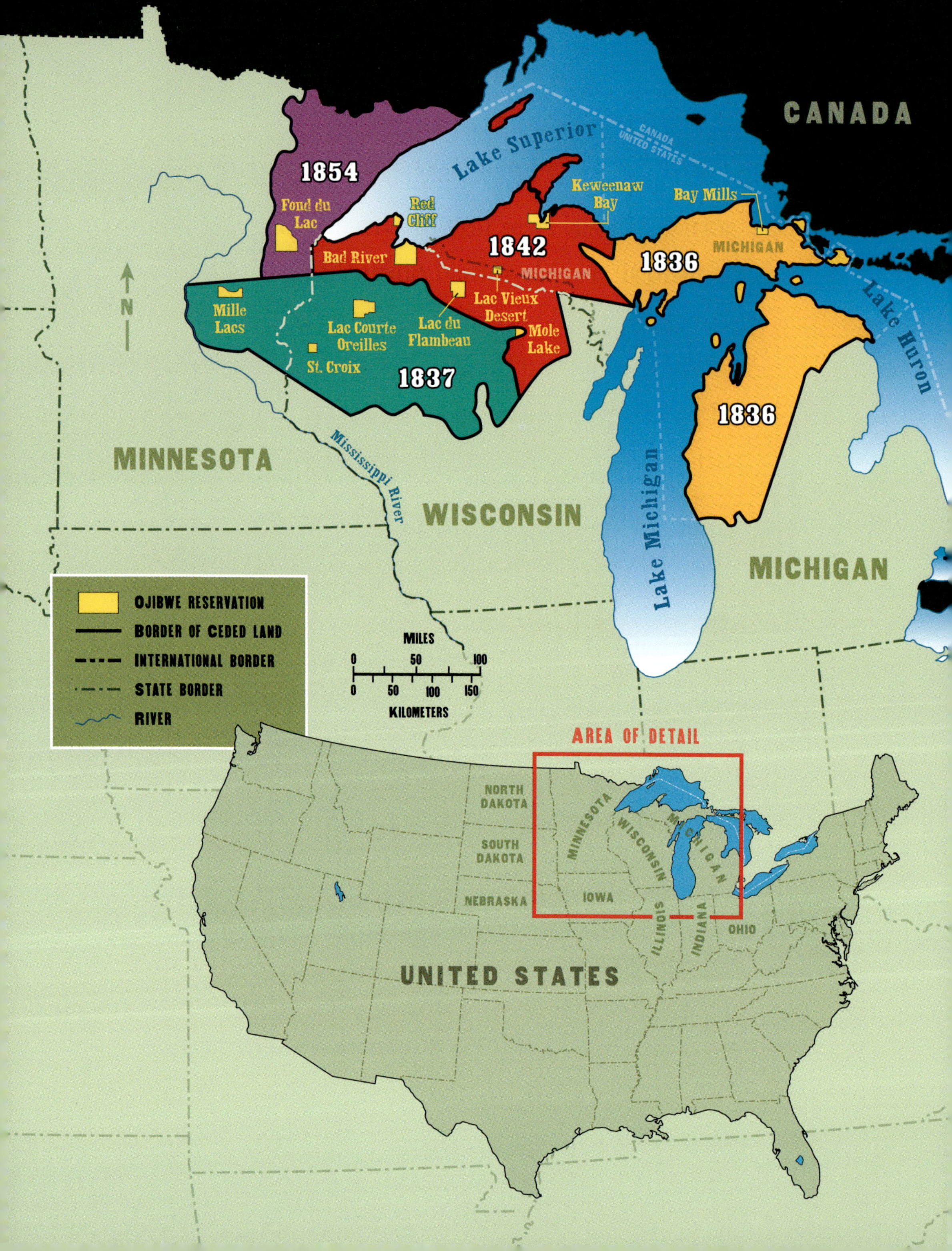

CANADA
Lake Superior
CANADA
UNITED STATES
1854
Fond du Lac
Red Cliff
Keweenaw Bay
Bay Mills
Bad River
1842
MICHIGAN
1836
MICHIGAN
Lac Vieux Desert
Mille Lacs
Lac Courte Oreilles
Lac du Flambeau
Mole Lake
St. Croix
1837
Lake Huron
1836
N
Mississippi River
MINNESOTA
WISCONSIN
Lake Michigan
MICHIGAN

OJIBWE RESERVATION
BORDER OF CEDED LAND
INTERNATIONAL BORDER
STATE BORDER
RIVER

MILES
0 50 100
0 50 100 150
KILOMETERS

AREA OF DETAIL
NORTH DAKOTA
SOUTH DAKOTA
NEBRASKA
MINNESOTA
WISCONSIN
MICHIGAN
IOWA
ILLINOIS
INDIANA
OHIO
UNITED STATES

In the 1850s, leaders of Native nations in the Pacific Northwest signed treaties that ceded their homelands. But these treaties, such as the 1855 Treaty of Point Elliott, also protected their rights to hunt and fish on those lands. The nations who signed this treaty were also promised a hospital and school. The 1855 Treaty of Point No Point also protected Native nations' rights to hunt and fish.

REFLECT

The US gained a lot of land in treaties with Native nations. Why do treaties still matter to the US?

Citizens of the Lummi Nation catch crabs in 2015.

These are just a few treaties signed between Native nations and the US. Native nations believe the US government should uphold the treaties that their ancestors signed. But not all nations were able to keep their treaty rights. And the government did not always keep its promises.

CHAPTER 3
Asserting Treaty Rights

Settlers and the US have not always upheld treaties with Native nations. In the late nineteenth century, state conservation officers began arresting Native peoples for hunting and fishing on and off reservations. In Wisconsin, two Ojibwe elders were arrested in 1897 because they had venison with them off the reservation. A few years later, Ojibwe men were arrested for setting fish nets even though they were exercising their treaty rights.

The officers argued that treaty rights did not apply on state land. They believed Native peoples should follow the hunting and fishing laws of the state, not the treaties. Native peoples argued that the treaties protected their rights to hunt and fish on these lands.

Despite the arrests, Native peoples across the US continued to practice the rights that were protected in treaties. They hunted and fished on ceded lands and on their reservations. Native peoples fed their communities. They honored the traditions of their ancestors.

Robert Satiacum (*right*) was a leader of the Puyallup Tribe. He advocated for Native fishing rights in the 1960s and 1970s.

Chief George Crows Fly High and Martha Grass (*center*) lead a protest advocating for Native fishing rights in 1968.

The Fish-In Movement

Native peoples exercised their rights throughout the twentieth century, even as state officers kept targeting them. During the Civil Rights Movement (1954–1968), Black people spoke out about how they were unfairly treated and advocated for their rights. Some protested by sitting in a place they were not allowed, such as a restaurant for

Ramona Bennett was a Puyallup Tribe leader who helped fish-ins gain national attention.

white people, and refusing to leave. They drew attention to their cause. This is known as a sit-in.

Nisqually, Puyallup, and Muckleshoot peoples were inspired by these sit-ins. In the 1960s, they decided to have fish-ins. Native people would gather and fish together. They wanted to raise awareness about their treaty rights and how those rights were being denied.

Native peoples continued to advocate for their rights. Finally, in 1973, a US judge upheld the 1855 treaties. These Native nations won and defended their treaty rights.

BILLY FRANK JR.

Nisqually activist Billy Frank Jr. (1931–2014) stood up for fishing rights. He was first arrested for fishing when he was only fourteen years old. By the 1960s, he had become an important figure in the Fish Wars of the 1960s and 1970s. Frank fought for treaty rights for the rest of his life before he died in 2014. After his death, he was awarded the Presidential Medal of Freedom in 2015.

Frank received many awards for his activism.

Ojibwe Activism

Ojibwe people in Michigan, Wisconsin, and Minnesota also fought for their treaty rights. In 1969 state officials said that Ojibwe people in Wisconsin could not fish in Lake Superior. But this went against what the treaties said. So men from the Red Cliff Band of Ojibwe in Wisconsin set gill nets, a wall of netting that catches fish, in Lake Superior. They were arrested the next morning when they pulled up the nets. The case

Richard Gurnoe was arrested for gill netting in 1969. His court case led to the *Gurnoe* decision.

A citizen of the Muckleshoot Indian Tribe shines a light on gill nets in 2006.

went to court. In 1972 the Wisconsin Supreme Court upheld their right to fish in Lake Superior. This is known as the *Gurnoe* decision.

In the 1970s, two Lac Courte Oreilles Ojibwe brothers were arrested for fishing off the reservation. This was the start of what is known as the Walleye War (1970s–1990s). It would take more than ten years for their rights to be upheld. But Ojibwe people persisted.

REFLECT

Native nations often use protests or the US court system to uphold their treaty rights. What similarities and differences do you see in the various actions Native peoples have taken to protect their rights?

Native nations stood up for their rights to continue hunting, fishing, and gathering. Protests such as the Fish Wars in Washington State and the Walleye War in Wisconsin show the strength and resilience of Native nations.

CHAPTER 4 Protecting Our Rights

Many Native organizations support Native nations in exercising their treaty rights. These organizations include the 1854 Treaty Authority, the Great Lakes Indian Fish & Wildlife Commission, and the Point No Point Treaty Council. These groups help protect animal and fish populations. They study the environment. They help educate Native and non-Native people about the importance of treaty rights.

Muckleshoot, Suquamish, Puyallup, Squaxin, Skokomish, and Nisqually peoples set out on canoes in 2017.

The Point No Point Treaty Council was established in 1974 after Judge George Boldt ruled in favor of the Native nations in the Pacific Northwest. The Point No Point Treaty Council helps protect natural resources. They help protect fish habitats. They monitor fish populations and decide how many fish can be caught each year. This helps stop overfishing. It also supports treaty rights.

Honoring Rights

Native nations celebrate and honor those who fought for their treaty rights. In 2024 Ojibwe people gathered on the Red Cliff Reservation in northern Wisconsin. They had a feast to celebrate the 1972 *Gurnoe* decision. They also honored the families of the people who had participated in the 1969 fishing protests.

RED CLIFF FISH COMPANY

The Red Cliff Fish Company opened in northern Wisconsin in 2020. It is run by the Red Cliff Band of Ojibwe. The fish company supports Chippewa people and the environment. Fishers make sure to only take what they need. Local people can buy fish to feed their families.

Fishers with the Red Cliff Fish Company supply local families with fish from Lake Superior (*above*).

REFLECT

Why are treaty rights important to the future of Native nations? How can these rights be protected?

Native peoples hunt and fish to feed their families. They hunt and fish to honor the ancestors who defended these rights through treaties. They hunt and fish to pass this knowledge down to future generations. It has not always been easy, but Native peoples proudly exercise their treaty rights. It is a celebration of their past, their present, and their future.

A member of the Tsimshian Haayuuk Dancers of Seattle welcomes salmon returning in 2003.

Glossary

advocate: creating awareness around an issue and campaigning for change. Many Native peoples advocate for their rights and protect their lands and resources.

assimilation: the process whereby individuals or groups of differing ethnic heritage are absorbed into the dominant culture of a society

cede: to no longer have control of something

extinct: no longer in existence

fish-in: a type of protest movement inspired by Civil Rights Movement sit-ins. At fish-ins, Native peoples fished to bring attention to the abuse of their treaty rights by state officers.

protest: a statement or an action that shows disapproval or objects to something. Protests can take many different forms, from sit-ins and fish-ins to marches and gatherings.

reservation: an area of land in the US that is held and governed by Native nations. In modern times, there are more than three hundred reservations in the US.

treaty: an official document signed between two or more sovereign nations

treaty rights: rights that Native nations in the US reserved or protected in treaties signed with the federal government

Learn More

Bellanger DeGroat, Cayla. *Native Lands and Sacred Places: Reclaiming and Protecting Native Lands*. Minneapolis: Lerner Publications, 2025.

Britannica Kids: Fish Wars
https://kids.britannica.com/kids/article/Fish-Wars/636175

Britannica Kids: US Treaties with American Indian Nations
https://kids.britannica.com/students/article/US-treaties-with-American-Indian-nations/635522

Craft, Aimée. *Treaty Words: For as Long as the Rivers Flow.* Toronto: Annick, 2021.

Native Knowledge 360: The Fish Wars
https://americanindian.si.edu/nk360/pnw-fish-wars#staging

Orr, Tamra B. *Native American History & Heritage: Ojibwe.* Mount Joy, PA: Curious Fox Books, 2024.

Washburne, Sophie. *The Story of the Native American Rights Movement.* Buffalo: Cavendish Square, 2024.

Wisconsin First Nations: Lifting the Nets
https://wisconsinfirstnations.org/lifting-nets-gurnoe-decision/

Index

Photo Acknowledgments

Image credits: Ecotrust (CC BY 2.0), p. 5; AP Photo/Elaine Thompson, p. 7; Brandon Bell/Getty Images, p. 8; Burton Historical Collection, Detroit Public Library, p. 10; U.S. National Archives and Records Administration, p. 12; Senate.gov, p. 13; Evan Abell/The Bellingham Herald via AP, p. 16; Museum of History and Industry, Seattle, p. 18; Bettmann Archive/Getty Images, p. 19; AP Photo/The News Tribune, Lui Kit Wong, p. 20; AP Photo/Ted S. Warren, pp. 21, 29; Wisconsin Historical Society, p. 22; JS Photo/Alamy, p. 23; GENNA MARTIN/San Francisco Chronicle via Getty Images, p. 26; Ali Majdfar/Getty Images, p. 27. Design elements: Miloje/Shutterstock; Archiwiz/Shutterstock; mikesj11/Shutterstock; kiwihug/Unsplash.

Cover: Farid Studio/Shutterstock; Yuliya_vector/Shutterstock.